CHARLIE BROWN'S CYCLOPEDIA

ELECTRICITY AND MAGNETISM
Invisible Forces

VOLUME · 13 ·

Based on the Charles M. Schulz Characters
Funk & Wagnalls

Charlie Brown's 'Cyclopedia has been produced by Mega-Books of New York, Inc. in conjunction with the editorial, design, and marketing staff of Field Publications.

STAFF FOR MEGA-BOOKS

Pat Fortunato
Editorial Director

Diana Papasergiou
Production Director

Susan Lurie
Executive Editor

Rosalind Noonan
Senior Editor

Adam Schmetterer
Research Director

Michaelis/Carpelis Design Assoc., Inc.
Art Direction and Design

STAFF FOR FIELD PUBLICATIONS

Cathryn Clark Girard
Assistant Vice President,
Juvenile Publishing

Elizabeth Isele
Executive Editor

Kristina Jones
Executive Art Director

Leslie Erskine
Marketing Manager

Elizabeth Zuraw
Senior Editor

Michele Italiano-Perla
Group Art Director

Kathleen Hughes
Senior Art Director

Photo and Illustration Credits:
The Bettmann Archive, 14, 36, 39, 44, 58; CQ Communications, Hicksville, NY, 49; E.R. Degginger/Earth Scenes, 18; Phil Degginger/Earth Scenes, 55; Larry Lee/West Light, 24; Lawrence Manning/West Light, 47; Chuck O'Rear/West Light, 28; John C. Stevenson/Earth Scenes, 26; Dick Thorn, 12, 17, 27, 31, 34, 40, 42, 45, 48, 51, 52, 56.

ISBN: 0-8374-0060-0

Part of the material in this volume was previously published in *Charlie Brown's Second Super Book of Questions and Answers*.

Funk & Wagnalls, founded in 1876, is the publisher of *Funk & Wagnalls New Encyclopedia*, one of the most widely owned home and school reference sets, and many other adult and juvenile educational publications.

INTRODUCTION

Welcome to volume 13 of *Charlie Brown's 'Cyclopedia!* Have you ever wondered how a light bulb works, or why batteries go dead, or how a picture appears on your television? Charlie Brown and the rest of the *Peanuts* gang will help you find the answers to these questions and many more about electricity and magnetism.

CONTENTS

CHAPTER 1

INVISIBLE ENERGY

Can you imagine a world without television and cassette players? Or what would everyday life be like without light bulbs and refrigerators? Or can you picture life without the telephone? A wonderful form of energy makes all these things work. It's the power of electricity and magnetism.

THE NATURE OF ELECTRICITY

What is electricity?

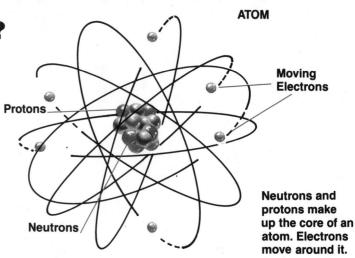

ATOM

Protons

Moving Electrons

Neutrons

Neutrons and protons make up the core of an atom. Electrons move around it.

Electricity is a form of energy. In order to understand electricity, you have to know something about atoms. Atoms are the tiny, tiny bits of matter that all things are made of. Atoms are so small that you can't see them even with the most powerful microscope. Though atoms are so small, they are made of even smaller parts. Some of these parts are called electrons (eh-LECK-tronz). When electrons move around among the atoms, a current of electricity is produced. In some materials, the electrons are loosely attached to the atoms. This makes it easy to break the electrons loose so they can move to other atoms. Electrons are loosely attached in all metals. That is why people use metal wires to carry electricity from one place to another. We say that these wires are good conductors, or carriers, of electricity.

What is static electricity?

When electrons do not move in a current, or flow, but get stored up, that's static electricity.

Sometimes when you walk across a rug, then touch a doorknob, you feel a small shock. Electrons move from the rug to your body and escape when you touch the doorknob. Then you feel the shock.

I'VE GOT IT FIGURED OUT, SIR.. WINTERGREEN CANDY MAKES SPARKS BECAUSE OF ELECTRICAL CHARGES..

WELL, CHEW HARDER.. I'M TRYING TO READ THIS MAP..

I DON'T THINK I HAVE ANY TEETH LEFT..

What is an electric shock?

An electric shock is what you feel when a current of electricity passes through your body. A strong shock, as from a light socket, can cause burns or even kill a person. A weak shock can sting your skin and make your muscles jerk.

Shocks are no fun, so here are some "nevers" to remember. Never touch electric things when they are wet, or if your hands are wet, and don't touch them if you are standing in water. Water is a good conductor, so wetness increases your chances of getting a bad—even a fatal—shock. *Fatal* means "causing death." Never climb telephone poles, and keep away from signs saying "Danger High Voltage." Stay away from electric wires lying on the ground. You don't have to be afraid of electricity. Just be careful with it.

Why are electric wires covered with plastic or rubber?

The plastic or rubber insulates (IN-suh-lates) the wire. This means it keeps the electricity from leaking out through the sides of the wire. An insulated wire is safe to touch. A bare wire can shock or even kill a person who touches it. Sometimes when a wire is old, the insulation cracks and starts to peel or break off. Spotting this is not always easy, but when it happens, someone might easily get a shock, or a fire might start. If you see a wire with cracked insulation, tell a grown-up so that the wire can be replaced.

What is a watt?

A watt is the unit used to measure electric power. A 100-watt light bulb uses 100 units of electric energy every second. A 60-watt light bulb uses 60 units of electric energy every second. In either case, electric energy is changed into heat and light energy. The watt is named after James Watt, the man who invented the steam engine.

What is an electric motor?

An electric motor is a kind of machine that is powered by electricity. The motor changes electric energy into movement that can do work. For example, an electric mixer has a small motor inside it. When the mixer is plugged in and the motor switch is turned on, the motor starts to spin. It causes the beaters to spin, too. The beaters then can mix up batter for a yummy cake.

How does electricity make toasters and electric irons get hot?

When a toaster or electric iron is turned on, an electric current flows through a coil of wire. This means that electrons are moving along among the atoms that make up the coil of the toaster or iron. As the electrons make their way, they bump into atoms. This bumping changes the energy of the current into heat energy. The coil becomes hot. Other appliances that use electricity to heat are electric coffeepots and hair dryers.

Magnetism and Electromagnets

What is a magnet?

A magnet is something that can attract iron. It can make a nail or a paper clip move toward it and then stick to it. A bar of iron or steel is an example of a simple magnet. Sometimes the bar is bent into the form of a horseshoe.

A magnet's attraction is strongest at its ends, or poles. Every magnet has a north pole and a south pole. If you hold two magnets near each other, the north pole of one will be attracted to the south pole of the other. If you try to bring the north pole of one magnet together with the north pole of another, they will repel, or push against, each other. This also happens with two south poles. Opposite poles attract each other. Poles of the same kind repel.

What do magnets have to do with electricity?

A lot. Magnetism and electricity are close relatives. In fact, electricity can produce magnetism, and magnetism can produce electricity.

A magnet has an invisible field, or area, of magnetic force around it. This is the area where the magnet's "pulling power" works. A wire with electricity running through it has the same kind of invisible magnetic field around it and the same kind of pulling power.

You can show the shape of a magnet's invisible field. Put a magnet under a piece of paper. Then sprinkle powdered iron on top of the paper. (You can probably get powdered iron at a hobby shop.) Now tap the paper gently. The iron will move into a pattern around the magnet. This pattern gives you a clear picture of a part of the magnet's invisible force field.

Do some magnets run on electricity?

Yes. They are called electromagnets. You can make a small electromagnet by winding lots of thin copper wire around an iron nail. Use wire that has a protective covering. Scrape off about an inch of the covering at each end of the wire. Attach the ends to a battery. You will have to have a friend hold the ends of the wire against the ends of the battery. It would be best to use the kind of battery called a lantern battery. You can get this kind of battery in a hardware store.

An electric current flows from the battery through the wire to the nail. The nail becomes magnetic. Now that it is magnetized, the nail can pick up other things made of iron.

If you disconnect the wire from the battery, the nail loses almost all of its magnetism.

The world's biggest magnet is 196 feet wide and weighs 40,000 tons!

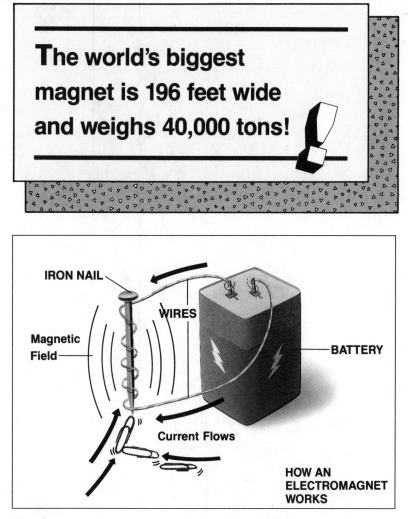

IRON NAIL

WIRES

Magnetic Field

BATTERY

Current Flows

HOW AN ELECTROMAGNET WORKS

Are electromagnets better than ordinary magnets?

In at least one way, yes. When an electromagnet is turned on, you can lift a heavy iron object and move it to any place you want. As soon as you shut off the electricity, the electromagnet will stop working. Then it will drop the iron.

You could not do this with an ordinary magnet. An ordinary magnet keeps holding on to iron things. That's why it is sometimes called a permanent magnet. *Permanent* means lasting forever. If you want to separate a piece of iron from a permanent magnet, you must pull it off.

This crane uses an electromagnet to lift junked metal.

How are electromagnets used?

Big electromagnets are often used in junkyards to load scrap iron into railroad cars. They are also used to separate iron from other kinds of scrap, such as aluminum, copper, or glass. Small electromagnets are used to make some machines work. For example, a doorbell uses an electromagnet.

CHAPTER 2

They can be lighter than a dime or too heavy to lift. They can be round, square, or shaped like a tube—and you can find them just about everywhere you look. They're in watches, the family car, flashlights, calculators, and many of your toys! What are they? Batteries!

CHARGE UP YOUR BATTERIES

BATTERIES

I THINK IT NEEDS A NEW BATTERY.

What is a battery?

A battery is something that produces an electric current with the help of different types of chemicals.

You've probably seen the type of battery that goes inside a portable radio or a flashlight. It looks something like a small can. This can and everything inside it is called a dry cell. Some batteries are made up of one dry cell. Others use two or more. Inside the cells are all the chemicals and other things needed to produce electric current.

The chemicals in dry cells are in the form of jellies or pastes. They can't be spilled. That's why these cells are called dry cells. There are also cells called wet cells. The chemicals inside these are liquids. Some batteries, called storage batteries, can be recharged and used over and over again. One kind of wet cell, a storage battery, is used to start a car. It is made of three or six cells in a heavy rubber or plastic box.

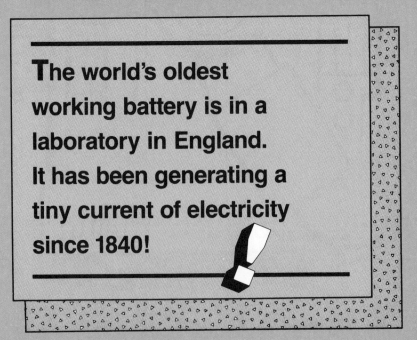

The world's oldest working battery is in a laboratory in England. It has been generating a tiny current of electricity since 1840!

How does a battery produce an electric current?

Batteries produce currents by a chemical reaction. Usually, a cell of a battery has three chemicals. One, called the electrolyte (eh-LECK-troe-lite), causes the other two to react. When the two chemicals react, the electrons in their atoms do a lot of moving around. One chemical ends up with a load of extra electrons. Another chemical ends up with a shortage of electrons. In this way, these two chemicals become what is called electrically charged. The chemical with extra electrons gets a negative, or minus, charge. The chemical with a shortage of electrons gets a positive, or plus, charge. When the chemicals are electrically charged, the electricity is ready to flow out of the battery.

In order for the flow to begin, there must be a complete path for the current to follow. Such a path is called an electric circuit (SIR-kit). A circuit is like a closed loop. When electrons travel along a circuit, they eventually go back to the place where they started. The electrons move around the circuit by using energy given to them by the battery. As you see in picture 1, the light bulb goes on when the circuit is complete. In picture 2, the light bulb does not go on because the circuit is broken.

What makes batteries go dead?

When a battery can no longer produce current, we say it is dead. A battery stops producing all current when its chemical reaction stops. The reaction stops when some of the chemicals have been used up.

IT'S ALWAY A GOOD IDEA TO CARRY EXTRA BATTERIES FOR WHEN YOU'RE EXTRA LOST.

Can a dead or weak battery be made to work like new again?

Ordinary flashlight batteries can't be renewed but certain other batteries can. These are called storage batteries. Renewing a battery is called recharging it. Cars have rechargeable batteries. Some electric drills, small vacuum cleaners, electronic calculators, and toys run on rechargeable batteries.

How are car batteries recharged?

Car batteries recharge automatically when the car's engine is running. The engine is connected to a type of generator, called an alternator. (We'll see how generators work in the next chapter.) The generator forces a current to run backward through the battery. This means the new chemicals change back into the old chemicals. The chemicals can react again to generate more electricity. Recharging is what allows the battery to keep starting the car every day for years.

CHAPTER 3

The flow of billions and billions of tiny electrons helps light our cities, heat our homes, cook our food, and clean our clothes Where does the flow of these electrons begin? Let's go with Charlie Brown and the *Peanuts* gang to find out.

GOING WITH THE FLOW

ELECTRIC CURRENTS

Huge plants like this hydroelectric plant generate enough power to light up whole cities.

Where do electric currents come from?

Most of the electric currents that people use come from batteries or from machines called generators. The current that runs the lights, the TV, the refrigerator, and other things in your house probably comes from a very large generator in a place called a power plant.

What is a generator?

A generator is a machine that makes electric current flow. A generator can be smaller than your big toe or bigger than your living room. A small generator can power a bicycle's headlight. A large one can give power to a whole city.

How does a generator produce an electric current?

A generator changes one form of energy into another. Every generator is run by something that turns or spins. The turning wheel of a bicycle runs the generator that powers its headlight. The spinning wheel or blades of a large engine run the generator. In the generator, the spinning energy is turned into electric energy. Here's how.

The people who make generators keep certain scientific facts in mind.

1. Around every magnet is an invisible force field.
2. If you move a coil of copper wire past a magnet, the wire cuts across the force field.
3. When the force field is cut by the wire, electricity flows through the wire.

Inside a generator are magnets (often electromagnets) and a coil of wire. The wire is usually wrapped around a rod called an armature (ARM-uh-choor). The engine that runs the generator moves the armature. As long as the armature keeps moving, the magnet's force field is cut. As long as the magnet's force field is cut, a current of electricity is produced, or generated.

POWER PLANTS

What is a power plant?

A power plant is a place where large amounts of electric energy are generated. There are at least seven different kinds of power plants. All of them have generators. The energy to run the generators, however, comes from different sources—oil, coal, atoms, water, gas, or wind.

The three most common kinds of plants are steam-electric plants, hydroelectric (hy-droe-ih-LECK-tric) plants, and atomic or nuclear (NOO-klee-ur) plants.

The Hoover Dam uses water to make electrical energy.

How does a steam-turbine plant work?

A steam-turbine plant uses steam to spin a turbine. The spinning motion of the turbine runs the generator that produces the electric current.

Steam is made by burning fuel to boil water. A huge amount of water is boiled to make steam. A steam-run plant is like a giant teakettle with steam blowing out the spout. The steam goes through a tunnel. Inside the tunnel are wheels with blades. This tunnel of blades is the turbine.

When steam blows through the tunnel, it makes the blades spin. The rod they are mounted on spins also. The rod is connected to the electric generators. When it spins, the generators run.

How does a hydroelectric power plant generate electricity?

A hydroelectric power plant uses a water-powered turbine to run a generator. The water comes from a reservoir (REZ-ur-vwar) or a lake. Most of it is held back by a large wall called a dam. Gravity, the force that pulls everything downward, makes some water flow through tunnels from the top of the dam to the bottom. Just before the water is let out at the bottom of the dam, it runs through the turbines and makes them turn. Flowing water can turn turbines just as wind can turn windmills or pinwheels. When turbines spin, they make the generators spin, and electric currents are produced.

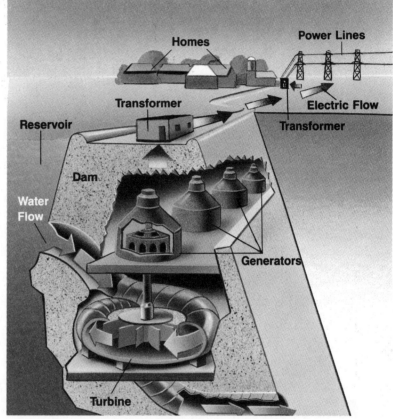

Homes

Power Lines

Transformer

Electric Flow

Reservoir

Transformer

Dam

Water Flow

Generators

Turbine

The world's largest hydroelectric power plant can make enough electric energy to turn on 64 million 100-watt light bulbs!

How does an atomic power plant generate electricity?

An atomic power plant works almost the same as a steam-turbine power plant does—it heats water. An atomic plant, however, doesn't burn coal, oil, or gas. Instead, it uses the metal uranium (you-RAY-nee-um) to make heat for boiling water. Instead of burning the uranium in a furnace, the uranium is put into a nuclear reactor. There, the atoms that make up the uranium split and produce huge amounts of nuclear energy. In doing this, a great amount of heat is given off. The heat turns the water to steam. The steam blows through turbines, and the turbines turn the generators.

Huge cooling towers are needed at this nuclear power plant in France.

BRINGING ELECTRICITY INTO HOMES

How does an electric current go from a power plant to people's houses?

It leaves the power plant through thick, heavy wires called transmission (tranz-MISH-un) lines. The current is sent out under high electrical pressure, or at high voltage. The lines are held up by tall metal towers.

Transmission lines stretch for miles. When they come to a town where people need electricity, some of the lines go into a place called a substation. The substation changes the high-voltage electricity into low-voltage electricity, which is safer. The low-voltage electricity then goes through wires from the substation to a transformer. This makes the voltage even lower. From there, it travels to houses, factories, and offices.

The same person, Michael Faraday, invented the electric motor, the generator, and the transformer!

PSYCHIATRIC HELP FEATURING LUCY

THE PSYCHIATRIST IS IN

I LOVE SEEING MY NAME UP IN LIGHTS!

What is a brownout?

Sometimes the area around a power plant needs more power than usual. This often happens in the summer, when people are using air conditioners. Sometimes one power district can buy power from a neighboring power district. Special cables are set up to make this possible.

If your power district cannot buy enough power from a neighbor, it may send out power to your home at a lower voltage. This is called a brownout.

If the voltage is reduced just a little, you won't notice it. If it is reduced 5 percent or more, your lights will be dimmer. Some appliances, such as your toaster and your iron, might not work as well as usual.

What is a blackout?

When the power plant stops sending electricity to your neighborhood, you have a blackout. During storms, if power lines are knocked down, you may have a blackout. Or, the power company may stop sending electricity to your area in order to send power to other places during a shortage. If something goes wrong at the power plant, there may be a blackout until the problem is fixed.

During a blackout, you can't watch TV or listen to the radio or stereo (unless yours run on batteries). Your refrigerator stops working, and if you have an electric stove, your parents aren't able to cook.

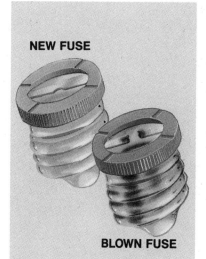

NEW FUSE

BLOWN FUSE

When a fuse filament melts, it breaks the connection and cuts off the flow of electricity.

A BLACKOUT! DOES THAT MEAN SUPPER IS OFF?

What does a fuse do?

It protects your house from fires caused by electric currents that are too large. All electric current that comes into your house must pass through the fuse. If you take the fuse out, the circuit is broken. No electricity comes in. If you put the fuse back, your house has current again.

Inside the fuse is a piece of metal. If this piece of metal gets too hot, it melts very quickly. Melting is the way it protects your house.

For example, suppose you are using an air conditioner, a TV, a toaster, and all the lights in your house. Then you turn on the microwave oven. You are now causing too much current to go through the circuit in your house. The wires become very hot, and they could start a fire. However, before this can happen, the metal piece in the fuse melts from the heat. We say that the fuse blew. Electrons can no longer flow through the wires of your house, so an electrical fire cannot start. In order to get electric current flowing into your house again, you must put in a new fuse.

Do circuits in all buildings have fuses?

No. Fuses are becoming old-fashioned. Newer buildings have circuit breakers instead. On the outside, circuit breakers look like ordinary light switches, but on the inside, a circuit breaker has a spring that bends when it gets hot. The spring will get hot if too much current is going through the circuit. If the spring gets hot and bends, the circuit breaker will flip to the off position. The current shuts off. After you wait a few minutes for the spring to cool, you can flip the circuit breaker back on. First, though, you should turn off some of your appliances. Then the circuit breaker probably won't switch off again.

How does the electric company know how much to charge each customer?

Each customer's house or apartment has a meter that measures how much electric energy the customer uses. The numbers on the dial tell the company's meter reader how many kilowatt-hours of electric energy the customer has used. A kilowatt is a unit of electric power. One kilowatt is equal to 1,000 watts. If you use a 1,000-watt iron for an hour, then you have used one kilowatt-hour of electricity. If you keep a 100-watt bulb burning for ten hours, that also adds up to one kilowatt-hour. The meter keeps track of every little bit of electric energy that is used, and it all adds up to a certain number of kilowatt-hours. Each month, a person from the electric power company comes to your house to read the numbers on your electric meter. This is how the company finds out how much power you have used. If you want to save money and energy, be sure to turn off lights, TVs, and other appliances when you're not using them.

CHAPTER 4

A BRIGHT IDEA

Flashlights, head-lights, night-lights, traf-fic lights. Lights in your house, in your school, on streets, and on highways. Without a doubt, lights make our world a brighter, safer—and more en-joyable—place to live!

LEMONADE
5¢ A GLASS

LIGHT BULBS

What makes a light bulb light up?

What makes the light go on when you flip a switch?

When you flip a switch, you complete an electric circuit. As long as the electrons keep flowing, the bulb stays lit. If you break the circuit by turning off the switch, the flow of electrons stops. Then the light goes out.

Inside a light bulb is a thin wire called a filament (FILL-uh-munt). When electricity passes through the filament, the filament becomes very hot. It becomes so hot that it glows and gives off a bright white light. The filament reaches a temperature of about 4,500 degrees Fahrenheit. The glass part of a light bulb keeps air from reaching the filament. It is important to keep air away from the filament because air has oxygen (OCK-suh-jin) in it. Oxygen is one of the three things needed to start a fire. The other two are heat and fuel, or something that can burn. A white-hot filament has the heat and is burnable. If any oxygen happened to reach a hot filament, it would burn up in an instant.

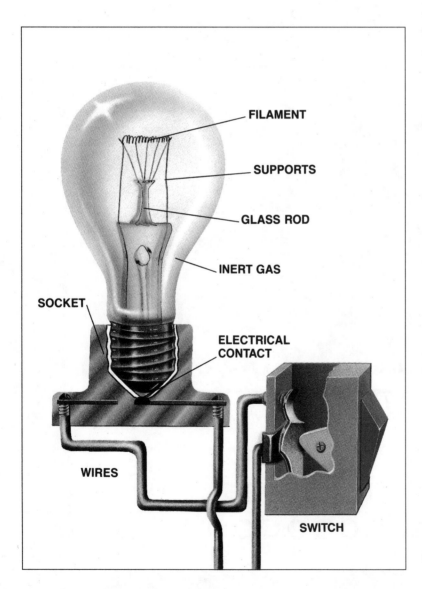

FILAMENT

SUPPORTS

GLASS ROD

INERT GAS

SOCKET

ELECTRICAL CONTACT

WIRES

SWITCH

It takes a switch, a socket, and wires to light a bulb.

What makes light bulbs burn out?

When a light bulb stops working, we say that it has "burned out," but it really hasn't burned. What really happened was that the bulb's filament broke. When the filament breaks inside a light bulb, electrons can't pass through it. When electrons can't pass through the filament, then the filament can't get white-hot and glow.

The oldest working light bulb has been burning in a firehouse in California since 1901!

Heat can make the filament break. Heat causes tiny cracks to form in the filament. The more you use the bulb, the bigger the cracks become. Finally, one of the cracks will stretch all the way through the filament, and the filament will break apart.

SOME OF US CAN'T SLEEP WITHOUT A NIGHT LIGHT.

Who invented the electric light bulb?

Thomas Edison, in 1879. He was one of the greatest inventors who ever lived. If you ask people to name some important inventors, usually the first one they will think of is Edison. His most famous inventions were the electric light bulb, the phonograph, and a motion picture machine called a kinetoscope (kih-NET-uh-scope). Altogether, he and his helpers invented more than 1,000 things.

Thomas Edison pictured in his laboratory

Thomas Edison's first electric light bulb glowed for 40 hours before it burned out!

MA'AM? THOMAS EDISON, HE WAS A MAN WITH A BRIGHT IDEA.

What is the difference between a light bulb and a fluorescent lamp?

The most obvious difference is their shape. A light bulb usually has a round or pear shape. A fluorescent (flow-RESS-unt) lamp usually has a tube shape. However, that is not the only difference.

In a light bulb, light is made with a glowing hot filament. In a fluorescent lamp, the glow comes from a special white coating (phosphor) on the inside of the glass tube. The coating glows whenever certain invisible rays, called ultraviolet (UL-truh-VYE-uh-lit) rays, hit it. These ultraviolet rays are made when you turn on the electricity. When the lamp is on, electrons shoot from one end of the tube to the other. The tube is filled with a special gas that gives off ultraviolet rays whenever electrons shoot through it. Fluorescent lamps save money because they use less electric power than light bulbs do.

What makes flash bulbs flash?

Oxygen. Flash bulbs have oxygen sealed inside. When you press the button on your camera, electric current flows through the bulb's filament. The filament glows. However, the glow doesn't last the way it does in an ordinary light bulb. This is because the oxygen makes the filament burn up in a flash of bright light. This flash gives you a lot of light in enough time to snap a picture.

Many modern cameras use a sealed glass tube that can flash over and over again and never wears out or burns out. This tube is called a strobe.

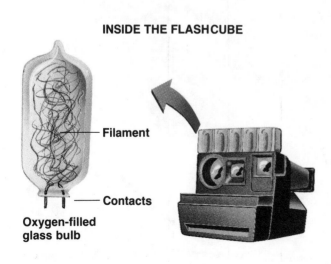

INSIDE THE FLASHCUBE

Filament

Contacts

Oxygen-filled glass bulb

Hundreds of years ago, people who lived far away from each other could not talk to one another. Letters had to travel by horse-back or boat, which could take days or even weeks. For shorter distances and faster delivery, they sent coded messages using flashing mirrors or smoke signals. Now, because of electricity, spreading important news is as easy as dialing a telephone.

SAY HELLO WITH ELECTRICITY

THE TELEGRAPH

Does electricity help people send messages?

Yes. If you want to contact someone far away, and you want to do it quickly, you can use a telegraph, a telephone, a cellular car phone, a CB radio, or even a fax machine. All these methods use electric energy.

What is a telegraph?

A telegraph is the oldest method of using electricity to send and receive messages. Samuel F. B. Morse invented the telegraph in 1837. For the first time, people could contact each other instantly between any two places that could be connected by wires. Before the telegraph, messages had to be sent by mail or by private messenger. The telegraph is no longer used much. It has been replaced by telephones and radios.

Samuel Morse demonstrates his invention, the electric telegraph.

How does a telegraph work?

Besides wires and batteries, a telegraph system has a sender, called a key, and a receiver, called a sounder. An operator works the telegraph.

The key is really just a switch the operator presses to make a current from a battery flow through the wires. When the operator stops pressing, the current stops. The sounder has an electromagnet that moves an iron lever when the current is on. When the lever moves, it taps or clicks against another piece of iron. The clicks are either long or short. Different patterns of clicks stand for different letters. The receiving operator listens to the clicks and can understand the message being sent. This system using clicks to stand for letters is called Morse code.

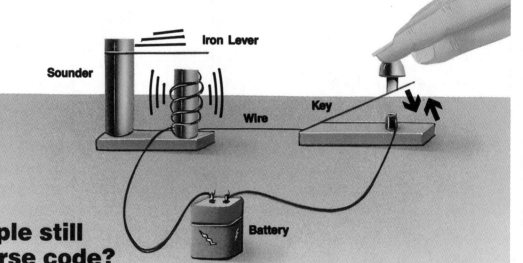

Do people still use Morse code?

Not usually. But a code much like Morse's is still used by radio operators. Instead of clicks, the radio code uses short and long beeps, called dots and dashes. If you know someone who operates a radio as a hobby, maybe you can listen to people sending messages in code. If you learn the code, you will understand what they are saying.

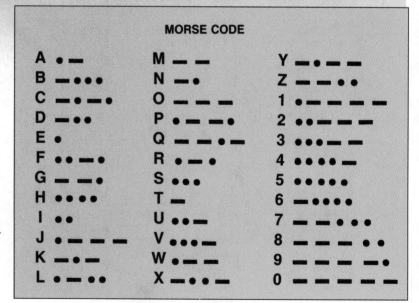

MORSE CODE

A	• —	M	— —	Y	— • — —
B	— • • •	N	— •	Z	— — • •
C	— • — •	O	— — —	1	• — — — —
D	— • •	P	• — — •	2	• • — — —
E	•	Q	— — • —	3	• • • — —
F	• • — •	R	• — •	4	• • • • —
G	— — •	S	• • •	5	• • • • •
H	• • • •	T	—	6	— • • • •
I	• •	U	• • —	7	— — • • •
J	• — — —	V	• • • —	8	— — — • •
K	— • —	W	• — —	9	— — — — •
L	• — • •	X	— • • —	0	— — — — —

Can you read this?

•••• • •—•• •—•• ———
••—• •—• ——— ——
—•—• •••• •— •—• •—•• •• •
—••• •—• ——— •—• —•

Write your name here, using Morse code.

_____

_____

Was there any fast way to send messages between America and Europe before telephones were invented?

Yes. In 1866, a heavy wire called a cable was laid across the bottom of the Atlantic Ocean. This cable made it possible for people to send telegraph messages between America and Europe. Before the cable was laid, messages had to go by ship. This meant that people didn't know what was happening on the other side of the ocean until days or sometimes even weeks later.

Now there are cables under all the world's oceans. They carry telephone messages and other electronic signals.

The longest undersea cable runs more than 9,000 miles from Australia to Canada!

THE TELEPHONE

How does a telephone work?

Every time you talk, you start sound waves moving through the air. When you talk on the telephone to a friend, the sound waves from your voice enter the part of the phone called the mouthpiece. The sound waves flow against a paper-thin piece of metal called a diaphragm (DYE-uh-fram). They make it vibrate, or move back and forth very quickly.

As the diaphragm vibrates, it jiggles tiny bits of carbon in a small box attached to it. The carbon bits move in time with the vibrations of your voice.

An electric current flows over the telephone wires between your house and your friend's house. The action of the carbon bits changes the strength of the electric current that goes over the wires. The current is strong when the carbon bits bunch together. It is weak when they spread apart. As a result, the spurts of current follow the same pattern as the sound waves from your voice.

When the spurts of current reach your friend's house, they must be changed back into the sound of your voice. In your friend's phone (and in yours, too) is a small electromagnet. When the spurts of current reach the electromagnet, another thin, metal diaphragm begins to vibrate. This diaphragm is in the part of the phone called the earpiece. The vibrations set sound waves in motion. The sound waves reach your friend's ear, and your friend hears you say "Hello!"

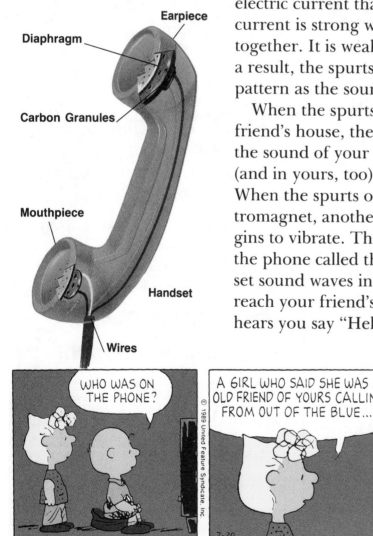

There are about 400 million telephones in the world! More than a third of them are in the United States!

SAY, DID YOU HEAR THAT CLICKING NOISE?

YEAH, CHUCK. WHAT DO YOU THINK IT IS?

The average American makes about 1,800 telephone calls each year!

Alexander Graham Bell invented the telephone in 1876 while trying (without success) to invent a hearing aid for deaf people!

HEE, HEE, HEE! I LOVE LISTENING ON THE EXTENSION!

THE RADIO

How does a radio work?

Radio is a way of sending voices and music through the air instead of along electric wires. It's like a wireless telephone. In fact, when radio was first invented, people called it the wireless. Instead of wires, radio uses electromagnetic waves. These waves can travel through air—and even through great distances in space.

OH, NO, A BEAGLE BLASTER!

Who invented the radio?

Guglielmo (goo-lee-YELL-moh) Marconi (mar-KOE-nee) invented the radio in 1895, when he was 21 years old. Marconi became very interested in science when he was a boy. He began experimenting when he was 16. For a long time, scientists had said it should be possible to make a radio—or wireless telegraph, as it was called—but nobody could figure out how to do it. Marconi studied other scientists' ideas and experiments. Then, when he was 20, he tried to invent a radio on his own. He built a transmitter that could send telegraph messages to a receiver across his attic—all without wires!

Guglielmo Marconi

Then Marconi successfully sent signals across his father's vegetable patch at home. Later he was able to send messages across England and the English Channel. In 1901, Marconi achieved an even greater goal: he sent the letter *S* in Morse code across the Atlantic, all the way from England to Newfoundland! Marconi's invention ushered in the amazing age of radio.

Early radio makers broadcast their own programs. If they hadn't, no one would have had a reason to buy a radio. There were no other programs to listen to!

RADIO WAVES

How are radio waves made?

Radio waves are made by a transmitter with the help of an antenna. A transmitter is a radio sender. The set you listen to is a radio receiver. The radio programs you hear are sent out by transmitters from radio-broadcasting studios, or stations.

A transmitter makes

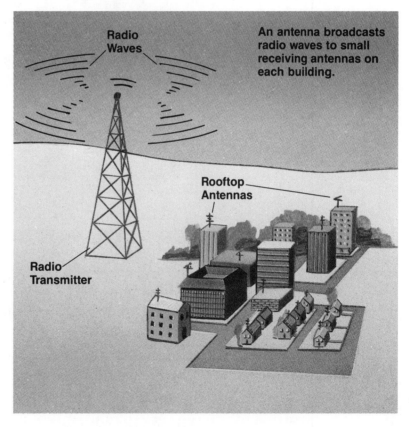

Radio Waves

An antenna broadcasts radio waves to small receiving antennas on each building.

Rooftop Antennas

Radio Transmitter

an electric current that vibrates very fast. It vibrates many thousands or even millions of times a second. Such a quickly vibrating current can flow through a wire. When it reaches the antenna, however, it changes form. Out of the antenna comes an invisible electromagnetic field that extends for miles. Sometimes it even reaches halfway around the Earth. This field is made of radio waves. These waves can be picked up by a receiver.

What does an antenna look like?

An antenna can be a piece of wire, or it can be a whole mass of wires hanging like a net from tall towers. Some antennas are metal poles or rods sticking straight up. Others are dish-shaped. The type of antenna used depends on how fast the radio waves are vibrating and on how far and in which direction you want them to go.

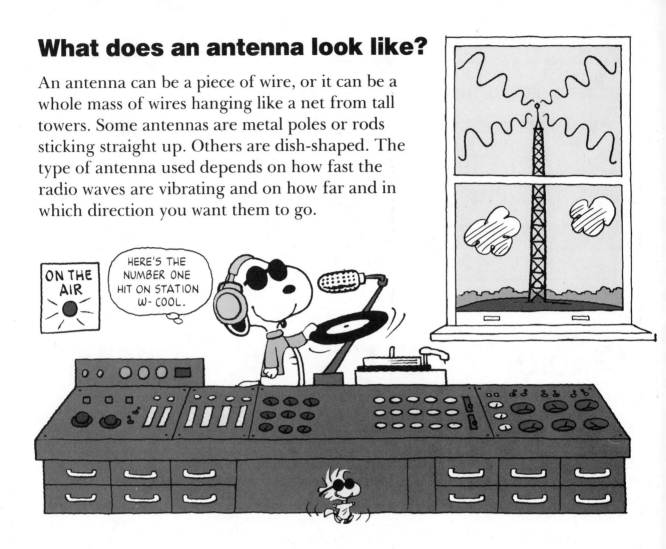

How do radio waves carry voices and music?

If you walked into a radio station, you would see someone talking into a microphone or playing music from a record, cassette, or compact disc. A microphone is much like the mouthpiece of a telephone. When you talk into it, sound waves cause a piece of metal in the microphone to vibrate. An electric current flows through the microphone. The current vibrates in time with the vibrations of voices or music. This current can travel only along wires, but the job of a radio station is to send this current out to radio receivers. The trick, then, is to get the microphone current to hitch a piggyback ride on the transmitter current. The combination can travel through the air or space as radio waves.

A radio transmitter has a part called a modulator (MOJ-uh-lay-tur). It mixes the microphone current with the transmitter current. In this way, the microphone vibrations can leave the antenna together with the transmitter's radio waves. That way the sounds travel through air as electric energy.

46

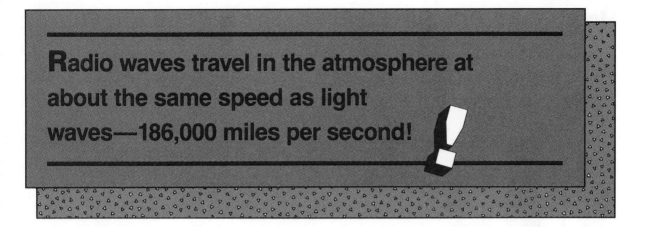

Radio waves travel in the atmosphere at about the same speed as light waves—186,000 miles per second!

Can radio waves be sent in a straight beam?

Yes. Most antennas send out radio waves in all directions. To send the waves in a straight line, you need a special antenna. This type of antenna is curved, like a dish. Radio waves come out in all directions from a rod pointing from the middle of the dish. Many of these waves then hit the curved part of the dish. The curve causes the waves to bounce back out, away from the dish. Then they travel in a straight beam.

Can a dish-shaped antenna receive radio waves?

Yes. Like most antennas, dish-shaped antennas can receive as well as send. Some, like radar antennas, send and receive at the same time. Dish antennas are very good for communicating with space satellites. They can be aimed directly at a satellite so that a clear, strong signal can be sent thousands of miles away. When receiving, a dish antenna picks up signals only from the direction in which it is aimed. The signal comes through very clearly.

A satellite dish can be used to receive radio signals from satellites orbiting the Earth.

How many radio-broadcasting stations are there?

The United States alone has about 9,000 radio-broadcasting stations.

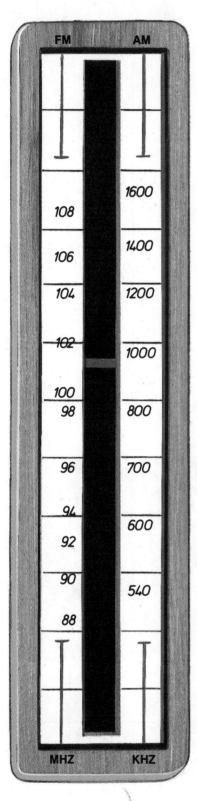

Why don't the radio waves from different stations get mixed up in the air?

When you play your radio, you turn the dial to a number. The number may be 700 or 1,000 or one of many other numbers. (There may be just a 7 or a 10 on your radio dial. If the radio is small, the zeroes will be left out.) Each number stands for a frequency (FREE-kwun-see). Each station broadcasts at a different frequency. The frequency is the rate of vibration of the waves that come from the station's transmitter. Your radio can "tune in" on the frequency you want to hear. Waves from other stations go by without being picked up.

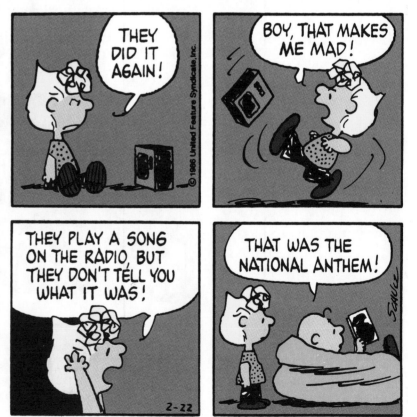

48

TALKING TO FRIENDS WITH RADIOS

What is a two-way radio?

A two-way radio is one that can send out radio signals and also pick them up. The radio you have in your house is a one-way radio. It only receives radio waves. The radio transmitter in a broadcasting station is also a one-way radio. It sends out radio waves.

A two-way radio is the kind you sometimes see taxicab drivers using. They talk into it to tell the cab company where they are taking you. They also get messages from the cab company through this radio.

People use two-way radios in boats, airplanes and other places without telephones.

What is a radio ham?

In spite of the name, a radio ham has nothing to do with food! It is a person who sends and receives radio messages as a hobby. Many boys and girls become radio hams. They send messages to other hams by code or by voice. There are special frequencies set aside for them to use. In order to send messages, hams have to pass a test and get a license. They also must have special equipment—a transmitter, a receiver, and an antenna. Many hams build their own equipment from kits. If you want to become a ham, the equipment will cost anywhere from 50 dollars to thousands of dollars.

A ham radio operator can communicate with people in other countries.

What is a CB radio?

CB stands for Citizens Band. It is a group of frequencies reserved for ordinary people to use. You do not need a license to use a CB radio. Usually, people have CB radios in their cars. Truck drivers use CBs a lot. They talk with other drivers and find out about traffic conditions. A special language has grown up among CB users. It is a kind of code. For example, *smokey* means policeman. *Rolling double nickels* means driving at 55 miles an hour.

CHAPTER 6

Have you ever wondered how your television makes a picture, or how music comes out of your stereo? Well, if you have, step right up and take a seat. The show is about to begin, with the *Peanuts* gang helping you tune in with electricity!

LOOK AND LISTEN!

WATCHING TELEVISION

How does black-and-white television work?

The screen that you look at is the front end of something called a picture tube. The screen is coated on the inside with a chemical (phosphor) that glows when it is hit by electrons. The electrons come from a part of the TV called an electron gun, at the back of the picture tube. If you use a magnifying glass to look closely at the screen while the set is playing, you can see lots of thin lines running across it. The electron gun fires a row of electrons along each line. Some places on the line are hit by a lot of electrons, and they light up brightly. Other places are hit by fewer electrons. These places appear light gray, dark gray, or black. The darkness depends on how many electrons hit them. When you look at all the light and dark spots together, your eyes see a picture. It's like looking at a photo-graph in a newspaper. If you look at the photo-graph closely, you can see that it is made up of lots of tiny dots.

Antenna

Screen

The image on a television screen is made up of tiny dots.

How does a picture get to your television?

A picture gets to your TV in much the same way that sound reaches your radio. Radio waves carry the video picture and sound from a transmitting station, through the air, to your TV.

How is it possible to see color on a TV?

Color television is very much like a comic strip or a color photograph printed in a magazine. The picture is a mixture of thousands and thousands of little colored dots (red, green, and blue). If you look at a color television screen very closely, you can see the little dots. When the set is off, the dots look gray or silvery. When the set is on, the dots light up.

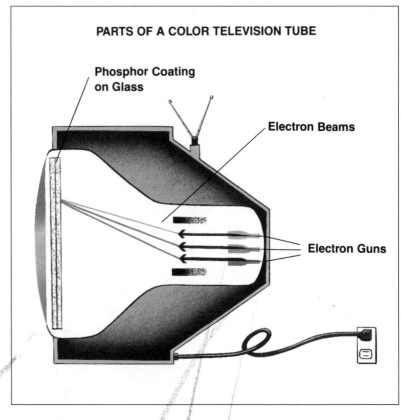

PARTS OF A COLOR TELEVISION TUBE

Phosphor Coating on Glass

Electron Beams

Electron Guns

The dots are made of a chemical (phosphor) that glows when hit by a beam of electrons shot from an electron gun. A black-and-white television set has only one electron gun. A color set has three, one for each color—red, green, and blue. Other colors—yellow, orange, purple, brown, black, and white—are made to appear on the screen by controlling how many red, green, and blue dots light up. For example, a picture of a glass of orange juice would be made up of a large number of red dots and a smaller number of green dots.

A color television camera separates everything it looks at into red, green, or blue. Then the television station transmits a red picture, a green picture, and a blue picture. The television catches these pictures with its antenna and sends the pictures to the three electron guns. The three pictures are mixed on the screen to show the same colors that the camera saw.

THIS PROGRAM WAS BROUGHT TO YOU AS A PUBLIC SERVICE..

CONSULT YOUR PAPER FOR A COMPLETE LISTING OF FUTURE PROGRAMS

AND NOW FOR A COMMUNITY REMINDER...

WAKE UP!

LISTENING TO MUSIC

What is a phonograph?

Phonograph is an old-fashioned word people once used to mean a record player or a hi-fi set. A modern phonograph is usually called a stereo.

What is hi-fi?

Hi-fi is short for *high fidelity*. Fidelity refers to how accurately a record or stereo set makes sounds. A high-fidelity recording of an orchestra should sound almost exactly like a real orchestra.

What does *stereo* mean?

Stereo means a sound-recording system that uses two or more microphones for recording and two or more loudspeakers for listening. Systems that record with only one microphone and play back with only one speaker are called monaural (mon-OR-ul), or mono for short. That means "one ear."

The extra microphones and loudspeakers used in a stereo system make the sound more realistic. When you listen to music on stereo, different sounds come from different loudspeakers. For example, you might hear a saxophone on one speaker and a guitar on the other. It sounds as though the musicians are right in the same room with you. Listening to a monaural record is almost like listening to live music with only one ear.

IT SOUNDS ALMOST AS IF BEETHOVEN WERE RIGHT HERE IN THIS VERY ROOM!

YOUNG PEOPLE'S CONCERT

YOU MEAN, HE'S NOT?

LUDWIG'S GREATEST HITS

MOZART PIANO CONCERTO

53

How is sound recorded?

Sound is recorded in two ways, called analog and digital. With the analog system, the current from the microphone makes a needle vibrate so that it cuts a wavy line on a plastic disc. The digital system does the same thing, but the vibrations of the needle are controlled by a computer. The computer takes the microphone current and changes it into tiny segments that, in turn, make the needle vibrate. The digital system gives an engineer excellent control of the sound being made. That way, when the record is played back, the sound is very close to what it was when it was being made live.

How does a phonograph record make sounds?

The surface of the record is covered with tiny grooves that are close together in a spiral. Seen under a microscope, these grooves have a wavy pattern that contains information about the sound that was recorded. When you place the phonograph needle onto a record that's rotating on a turntable, the needles vibrate as it follows the "wiggles" in the groove. This needle has a magnetic field around it. As the needle moves across the field, it makes an electric current that varies. This current is changed to sound in the loudspeaker, just as the electric current in a telephone becomes sound in the phone's receiver.

A CD player uses a laser light to read compact discs.

What is a compact disc player?

A compact disc (CD) player is a musical device that plays compact discs instead of records. The first thing you notice about a compact disc is that it has no grooves as a phonograph record does. Rather, it is a very thin disc of plastic. No needles are used to play it. Instead, a tiny laser beam in the CD player below the disc reflects off the sound track to a light detector. This light detector then changes the light to electric current for the loudspeaker.

The sound is recorded on the disc by the digital method. A digital computer puts a series of tiny holes into the disc. These holes represent the actual computer code. When the code is played back on the CD player, the code tells the computer in the player which sounds to send to the loudspeaker. When the current gets to the loudspeaker, it is changed back to sound.

The compact disc is better than other recording systems for several reasons. No needle is used with it, so the disc is not worn out by the needle. Also, using computers, it is easier for recording companies to make changes in the kind and quality of the sounds that are recorded on a CD. In fact, the control is so great that a recording can be made without a microphone. The recording engineer merely types the desired code into the computer, and the computer directs the making of the "pits" on the plastic.

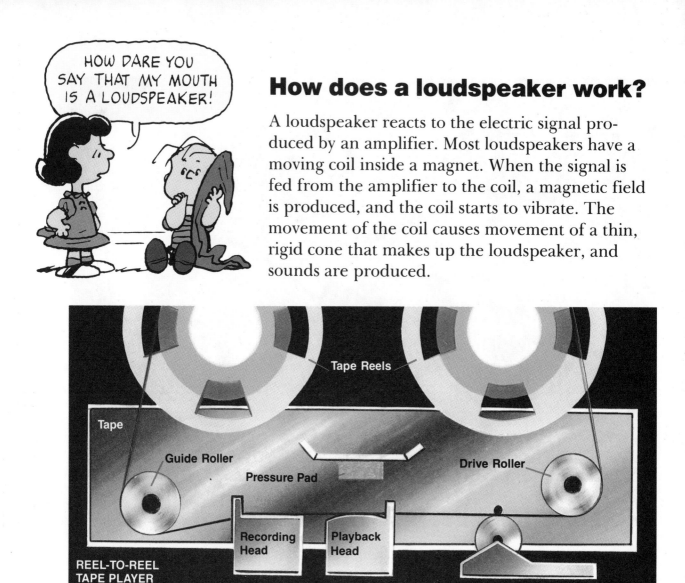

HOW DARE YOU SAY THAT MY MOUTH IS A LOUDSPEAKER!

How does a loudspeaker work?

A loudspeaker reacts to the electric signal produced by an amplifier. Most loudspeakers have a moving coil inside a magnet. When the signal is fed from the amplifier to the coil, a magnetic field is produced, and the coil starts to vibrate. The movement of the coil causes movement of a thin, rigid cone that makes up the loudspeaker, and sounds are produced.

Tape Reels

Tape

Guide Roller

Pressure Pad

Drive Roller

Recording Head

Playback Head

REEL-TO-REEL TAPE PLAYER

How does a tape recorder work?

By magnetism. The tape is a plastic ribbon coated with a chemical—iron oxide or chromium (KROW-me-um) oxide. Each bit of the chemical is like a tiny magnet. Inside a tape recorder is an electromagnet called a recording head.

When you speak into a tape recorder's microphone, electric waves from the microphone go into the tape recorder. They cause vibrations in the field around the electromagnet. As the tape passes through the electromagnet's field, the bits of chemical on the tape are magnetized into different patterns. These patterns are a recording of the sound waves of your voice.

When you play back the tape, the patterns on it affect another electromagnet called a playback head. This electromagnet makes faint waves or signals that go into an amplifier. The amplifier makes the signals stronger. The strong signals make a loudspeaker vibrate. The sound vibrations that come from the speaker are just like the ones that went into the microphone.

Does a video recorder work like a tape recorder?

Yes. Video, or picture, recorders record both pictures and sound, but they work in very much the same way as tape recorders. A video recorder takes the video and audio, or sound, signals from the TV and saves them on a magnetic tape, which is similar to the tape used in a tape recorder. The videotape is larger than an audio tape because it must store information about the color and brightness of the picture, as well as the sound. The video information is stored on tracks along the tape—the same way that sound is stored.

Are there disc players for television?

Yes. There are video laser discs for movies and television. The laser disc is a digital device and can hold more information than a video-cassette tape, so the picture is more detailed and is better. The laser disc looks like a compact disc, but it is larger.

DID YOU KNOW...?

• Different appliances use different amounts of electricity. For instance, the energy used by a 100-watt light bulb in ten hours can keep an electric clock going for three months.

IS ANYBODY THERE?

Alexander Graham Bell

• The fastest train on record is electric. It is a French train called the TGV. TGV stands for *très grande vitesse* (TRAY GRAHND vee-TESS). That means "very great speed." On February 26, 1981, the TGV hit an all-time high with a speed of 236 miles per hour.

• The first words Alexander Graham Bell spoke into his new invention, the telephone, were "Mr. Watson. Come at once. I want you." He had spilled battery acid on his pants and needed his assistant's help quickly!

• According to legend, magnetism was first discovered by a Greek shepherd named Magnes. Shepherds carried wooden staffs with iron tips to help them climb hills when they were herding their flocks of sheep. Magnes noticed that sometimes the iron tip on his staff picked up pieces of black rock that stuck to the iron tip of the staff.

The black rock became known as magnetite. Before long, all the shepherds knew about the magic of magnetite, and they spread the news of this amazing discovery throughout the world.

• Early sailors used magnetite to make compasses. They found that the same end of the magnetite always pointed in the same direction—north. After that, the sailors did not need the Sun and stars to guide them. These sailors called their compasses lodestones. The word *lode* means "to lead," and that's just what the compasses did—they led the way!

SO, WHO FORGOT THE COMPASS?

◆ IN THE ◆
NEXT VOLUME

Have you ever wondered how cloth is made, or why queens wear crowns, or what a zoot suit is? You'll find the answers to these questions and lots more in volume 14, *Clothes from Head to Toe—What We Wear and Why.*

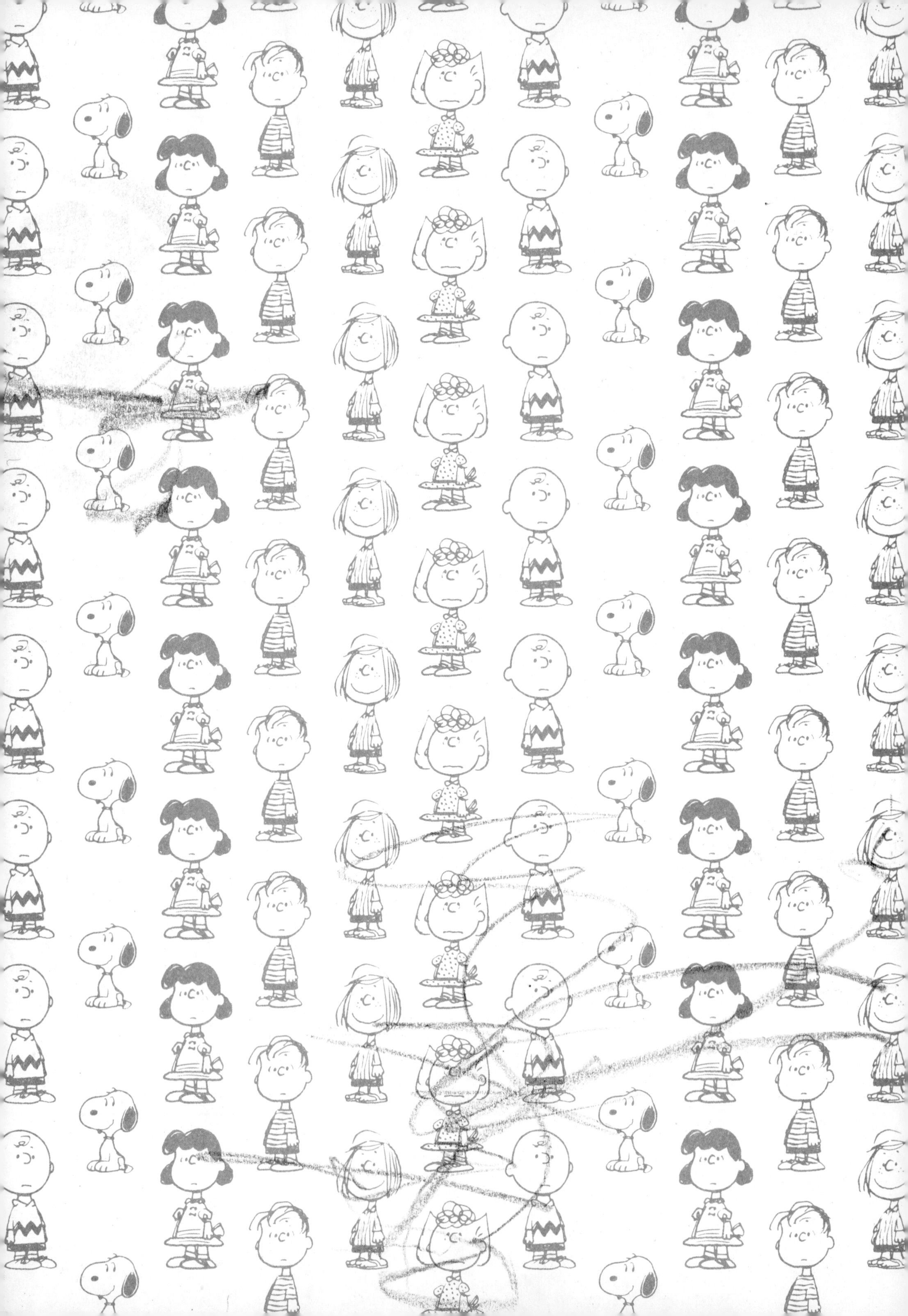